M000028465

Ms. Quirk eloquently walks us through the decision-making level of all issues that arise in the divorce process--from contemplation of ending the marriage through the final decree.

Presented in an orderly and concise manner, this little book covers all the questions you have and those you have not yet thought of. --Betty Hedrick CFP® CDFA®, The Hedrick Co.

Finally, a great book on divorce for grownups! Quirk's book is informative and empowering. Let her guide you and your spouse through your divorce peacefully! Quirk takes the sting out of divorce and focuses on cooperation which saves you money and pain! -- Shirin Sherkat, Psy.D., Parent Strategist, Author & Speaker, Founder of *Create Happy Kids*

If you are facing a divorce, Karin is the epitome of the profession—a family law attorney of the quality you can usually only dream of. She has a vast knowledge of the divorce landscape and the wisdom that only years of experience can bring. She will help you summon your inner adult, for divorce is an adult adventure, but also support you through the process with a kind heart and compassion. --Gregory Lease, Personal Divorce Coach

Six-Word Lessons for a Peaceful Divorce provides a clear and easy to follow outline of the possible routes divorce can take in Washington state. Although not all the information presented in this book will be relevant to each individual's situation, Karin Quirk does an excellent job of answering questions that may come up whether someone is thinking about separation, hoping to avoid it, or are already in the middle of a divorce. Highly recommended. --D, client

Six-Word Lessons for

A PEACEFUL
DIVORCE

100 Lessons to Dissolve
Your Marriage with
Respect and Cooperation

Karin Quirk, Esq.

Published by Pacelli Publishing
Bellevue, Washington

Six-Word Lessons for a Peaceful Divorce

All rights reserved. No part of this book may be reproduced or transmitted in any form or by any means, electronic or mechanical including photocopying, recording or by any information storage or retrieval system, without the written permission of the publisher, except where permitted by law.

Limit of Liability: While the author and the publisher have used their best efforts in preparing this book, they make no representation or warranties with respect to accuracy or completeness of the content of this book. The advice and strategies contained herein may not be suitable for your situation. Consult with a professional when appropriate.

Copyright © 2017 by Karin Quirk

Published by Pacelli Publishing
9905 Lake Washington Blvd. NE, #D-103
Bellevue, Washington 98004
PacelliPublishing.com

Cover and interior designed by Pacelli Publishing
Cover image by Pixabay.com
Author photo by Tara Gimmer

ISBN-10: 1-933750-69-3
ISBN-13: 978-1-933750-69-9

For John Wesley, who knows his three grammas love him very much, and his mom and dad, Kathleen and Doug

Table of Contents

Acknowledgements

I want to express my appreciation to my tribe that has offered support and encouragement. My Entrepreneur Accountability Group (EAG) nudged me along, as did my book coach, Karen Lynn Maher. Patty Pacelli, my publisher, has been patient and supportive. I also want to thank my Front Seat Squad for pushing me across the finish line.

Introduction

I'm often asked why I chose family law. My reply is that it chose me. I've always been interested in people and their relationships--their hopes and dreams. As I began my law practice I tried a number of practice areas but always ended up helping people with their divorces. Soon it became apparent that this would be my area of focus. After many years in the trenches, I developed the sincere belief that there must be a better way. I studied divorce mediation, collaborative law and nonviolent communication. Thus I developed *Divorce for Grownups*.

Not all divorces are amicable but in my practice I always start out that way. One can ramp up, but once all the bad things have been said and the nasty declarations have been filed with the court, it is more difficult to pursue a cooperative path.

Hopefully you will find this information useful. Armed with knowledge, you can make better decisions for your children and for your own future.

Note: to the extent my inner grammar nerd will let me I have attempted to be gender neutral. I've made every attempt to avoid stereotypes. Men and women care equally about their children and traditional roles are often reversed. Furthermore, I try to refer to "spouse" rather than "husband" or "wife." Marriage equality is the law in all states now and we are learning to modify our forms to match.

Disclaimer: Nothing in this book should be interpreted as legal advice. Laws differ in every state. I am licensed in Washington State and at one time practiced in California. It is critical that you seek legal advice in your jurisdiction.

I am happy to answer questions but must limit my responses to residents of Washington State.

You may contact me at
Karin@divorceforgrownups.net.

Ending Marriage; not an Easy Decision

1

Trial separation, is there still hope?

Sometimes it is good to just get away from each other for awhile. There is no need to do anything "legal." A vacation from each other might help you decide. Be sure to communicate to your spouse that you are not terminating the marriage at this time, and do not leave without parenting arrangements in place.

2

Legal separation, is it for me?

A legal separation is an alternative to divorce. All issues regarding property and children are resolved just like a divorce except the parties are not free to marry. The parties can file taxes separately. Generally, the spouse is not eligible for spouse's health insurance. The most common reason for legal separation is religious beliefs.

3

Does it matter who files first?

There is no legal significance as to who files first. Many couples choose to file the equivalent of a joint petition. For some it is a statement that you are truly serious about ending the marriage. Sometimes a reluctant spouse does not want to file but will "go along." If both file, the court will use the earlier filing number.

4

Do I have to have grounds?

In Washington State, the only grounds for divorce is, "The marriage is irretrievably broken." Some states cite "irreconcilable differences." Every state now has some version of "no-fault" divorce but requirements differ. If one party wants a divorce, it will happen. You cannot object to the divorce itself, merely the financial and parenting issues.

5

Moving out: do I lose rights?

You do not lose your rights to property or possessions by moving out. Merely moving out is not "abandonment." Do not move out without a plan for the children. Telling your spouse that you will get the children when you have an adequate place to stay can work against you. Temporary arrangements can easily become final.

6

What does *no-fault* mean anyway?

No-fault means that you do not need to provide reasons for the divorce other than the irretrievably broken language or irreconcilable differences of some states. *No-fault* also applies to support and financial issues. Except for rare exceptions, who did what to earn or spend the money is not relevant.

I do not want a divorce.

While laws may differ in some states, in Washington State, one cannot contest a divorce. Your best option is to focus on getting the most reasonable settlement you can. Of course, you can ask for a "cooling off" period or even attend counseling but ultimately if one spouse has made the decision to divorce, the other has no other option.

8

My spouse is having an affair.

While this may be devastating to you, keep in mind that not every couple dealing with infidelity gets a divorce. Some marriages survive with counseling. From a legal perspective, an affair is not relevant either to the financial settlement or the parenting plan. An exception can be made if your spouse spent an inordinate amount of community assets on his affair.

9

I'm staying because of the kids.

Some people feel an obligation to stay in a marriage because they feel they must for the benefit of the children. Child development experts will tell you this is not beneficial for anyone, including your spouse, you, and the children. If you are worried you won't be able to support them financially, a lawyer will explain support obligations. Who makes the money is never the issue.

10

I don't know my spouse's location.

While it is more complicated, it is possible to divorce a person whose location is unknown. There are various notice procedures that require court orders. Sometimes one can send certified mail to a last known address or sometimes notice in a newspaper is permitted. Legal assistance is crucial in this instance but it can be done.

Build Your Team, Make a Plan

11

Tell family how to support you.

You are making the decision to dissolve your marriage. Your family may want to support you but they don't know what you need. Let them know. Ask them to respect your decisions and that you are not asking them to be involved. You may need financial assistance or temporary housing but don't give up your own power.

12

Know which friends to confide in.

Your friends will want to take your side. Remember they are seeing things through their own lenses and experience. What was appropriate for them may not be relevant to your situation. Be discreet with who you confide in, especially if there are things you don't want to get back to your spouse. Show extra restraint with social media!

13

Take charge of your own life.

Maybe for the first, second or third time in your life you are making your own decisions. Pay attention to your feelings. Where do you want to live? What do you want your future to look like? Try some new activities, meet new people. Make it a new adventure. Don't make divorce your only occupation.

14

Do your research to be informed.

Research your state's laws regarding divorce, property, support and parenting. Washington State has a good official website as do many states. Proceed with caution on sites selling you something. Make sure a website or blog is relevant to your state. Check the writer's credentials. Don't get legal advice from nonlawyers. Blogs from lawyers in your community are a way to gauge their perspective.

15

Be wary of well-intentioned advice.

Your hairdresser's cousin is not a good source of information. Your neighbors and friends have opinions based on their own experience which may be vastly different from your situation. Neighborhood forums can be a particularly poor source of information. Most lawyers will answer questions with "It depends." Your case is unique to your facts.

16

Get thee to a financial planner.

A certified divorce financial analyst (CDFA) can help you plan your budget and make wise financial decisions about a property division. You can often save attorney fees if your CDFA has prepared spreadsheets and proposed possible scenarios. She can also help make sure all assets have been accounted for. A CDFA is not an investment advisor.

17

Do not try to hide money.

You've been squirreling away a little money each month because someone told you to have a little nest egg "just in case." You must disclose all funds. Even if you had an inheritance you consider to be your separate funds, you must disclose. If you own your own business, don't try to hide money by keeping it in the business account.

18

Playing private detective: is there need?

You are suspicious of your spouse so you play private detective because you really want proof. What will you do with this proof? It is a no-fault state and the court is not interested. Maybe it is time for an adult conversation. Discuss your suspicions. Maybe consider marriage counseling. If the marriage is over, you don't have to prove fault.

19

Start gathering all your financial information.

Gather tax returns, pay stubs and account statements. Get a copy of your credit report and auto values. You may also want to save utility and household bills as well as track your usual expenditures. This will help as you work on financial issues. Do not think, however, that you must have all the financials in place to start your case.

20

Do you really need a lawyer?

If you have been married less than three years, own no property, have no debt and no children, then you could do it yourself, but a lawyer may be able to point out hassle-free, low-cost options. If you have children, own a house, or have investments, you must at least consult with an attorney.

Your Lawyer is Your Biggest Decision

21

How do I find a lawyer?

The lawyer who does your will or handles your business matters is most likely not a divorce lawyer but knows of someone who has a good reputation. Stick to lawyers who focus on family law. Check out the lawyers' websites to get an idea of the ideology. "We fight for you" or "We offer amicable divorces" can offer clues.

22

I have no money, now what?

Does your spouse control all finances and you can't access any money? You can file a motion for temporary orders with the court. Most lawyers will ask for a deposit, however. Perhaps a new credit card or a loan from friends of family can help. If you are truly a low-income person, there are legal clinics available.

23

How much does a lawyer charge?

Most lawyers charge by the hour but will want an upfront deposit. Your costs probably will exceed the deposit. There is a new trend toward all-inclusive flat fees, with caveats for trial or extraordinary costs. Clients like this because they are not billed for every phone call and email and the cost is predictable.

24

Can my friend the lawyer help?

Unless your friend is a divorce attorney, probably not. Your friend can help you find a lawyer but family law is complex and most lawyers limit their area of practice. Also, a lot of family law is not necessarily in the books and there are a lot of emotional issues that experienced family law attorneys are trained in.

25

What about all those online forms?

If you have been married under three years, have no assets, debt or children, this could be an option. Children, real estate, and retirement accounts make things more complex. The questions may seem simple but the way you answer them can make a significant difference. Also, lawyers can help you keep personal information private. Lawyers have professional software also.

26

Can I get a contingent fee?

A contingent fee is one in which the lawyer gets a percentage of what you are awarded and you do not pay an upfront fee. This is most often done in personal injury cases. In the state of Washington and probably most states, it is unethical to charge a contingency fee in a divorce case.

27

Retainer, flat fee, hourly... what difference?

A retainer is a monthly fee you pay for a lawyer to be available to you. Such arrangements are rare. Generally, you pay a deposit. The lawyer bills hourly against the deposit and you are asked to refresh the deposit when it is used up. A flat fee is an amount you pay for a specific scope of work, such as divorce.

28

How does a flat fee work?

A flat fee is generally paid up front and covers all or a specific part of a case. You are not billed for phone calls, emails or consult time. All documents are included. The fee agreement is very specific about what is covered and what extra costs might be. People like it because they can budget just what their divorce will cost.

29

Should you hire an aggressive lawyer?

A very aggressive lawyer generally means you'll spend more money and have a miserable time. What you want is an effective lawyer. A lawyer skilled in mediation and negotiation can get you better results for less money and less emotional trauma. You do not need a grandstander who puts on a show for your benefit. It does not impress the judges.

Ready to Start the Divorce Process

30

Delayed filing, does it make sense?

Sometimes people delay filing a case until all the details are worked out. This is not necessary. You may want to delay filing if you are trying to obtain a mortgage or loan. Filing a petition for divorce is public record and will show up on any public record check. Sometimes there are immigration issues.

31

Preserve your privacy, don't tell all.

The divorce petition is a public record available for anyone to see. You do not need to put your financial details in the petition. "To be determined" is an acceptable answer. You do have to list your children's names and dates of birth as well as your date of marriage and birthdates.

32

Joinder, co-petition: you set the tone.

If you file a petition, you also must serve a summons. This alone sets an adversarial tone. You can ask your spouse to sign a "joinder" which means you both are agreeing to the divorce even if you don't agree on terms. An even more congenial process is to file a co-petition, which some attorneys will help you with.

33

How to determine date of separation

The date of separation (DOS) can have important consequences. Unless the date is very clear you should not commit to a date on your initial pleadings. Financial accounts are valued by DOS. This can make a huge difference. You and your attorney should determine this date after you have considered all facts.

34

Plan ahead if you expect default.

If you do not expect your spouse to respond at all, you may do the divorce by "default." This is often done when you do not know your spouse's whereabouts. It is important that you list everything you are asking for in the initial petition, including financial division, parenting and child support.

35

Can you avoid the filing fee?

In Washington State, there is a provision for waiving a filing fee if your income falls below a certain amount. You need a special court order. Sometimes the filing fee is waived or it may be delayed. Once it is determined that you are getting a financial settlement, you may be required to pay the fee then.

36

What if you can't find spouse?

It is possible to serve an individual by mail at their last known address but you must get a court order. If you do not have an address, you must show that you have tried to locate the person and you would get a court order to serve by publication in a paper. This can take a long time and should be a last resort.

37

Does it matter who files first?

The person filing is the Petitioner. The other party is the Respondent. There is really no legal significance. Some people feel there is an emotional difference--they don't want to be the one filing or the other way around. Technically, if there is a trial, which is rare, the Petitioner presents the case first.

38

Temporary order to preserve status quo

If you are concerned about your spouse moving money, closing accounts, or running up debt, you may want to get temporary financial restraints. This would also mean maintaining utilities, health insurance, cell phones and other ordinary living costs. Some jurisdictions have automatic financial restraints. Money can be spent "in the ordinary course of business or personal expenses."

39

Temporary orders for safety and sanity

If you are concerned about your physical wellbeing you will want to consider temporary no-contact orders. They can prevent your spouse from coming to your home or place of employment, or contacting you at all by phone, text, or email. You may also have your spouse required to leave the home so you have exclusive use.

40

You have been served, now what?

If you have been asked to acknowledge receipt of documents, go ahead. You are not agreeing to anything, merely acknowledging you got them. Avoiding service will not give you any advantage. Confer with a lawyer as there are certain deadlines to meet. Be sure and check if there are any upcoming hearings for temporary orders.

Children and Divorce Can Be Complicated

41

Telling the children about the divorce

Ideally you should tell the children together. Let them know Mom and Dad are no longer going to live together but Mom and Dad both love them. Help the children know it is not their fault. Some couples like to have the children pick furniture or paint colors for their new room, or involve them in other decision that will affect them.

At what age do children decide?

Many people have the mistaken notion that there is a certain age at which children get to decide where they live. Children should never ever be involved in this process. In Washington State, the age of majority is eighteen. Children will tell each parent what they think they want to hear. Don't involve them.

43

Words matter,
it is not custody.

Children are not property to be divided. We use the term "parenting plan" advisedly. Also, you do not "visit" your children. We call it parenting time or residential time. The plan needs to account for the children's school schedule, the parents' work schedule and the geographic distance of the two homes. Avoid use of percentages even if some court documents refer to such.

44

Parenting plan for children's best interest.

The standard for parenting plans is "best interest of the children." Parents should put aside their egos and truly consider what is the best interest of the children. The goal is to consider the children's individual needs and maintain as much stability as possible. Rarely should a plan separate siblings, but in rare cases, with the help of a counselor, this may be the best choice.

45

Accommodating the different lifestyles of parents.

Sometimes a parent may be upset by the other parent's lifestyle and does not want the children exposed. This is especially true if one parent is now in a same sex relationship. The parent may feel angry or betrayed. The only questions to ask are, "Is this a loving home for the children?" and, "Are they safe?" Then learn to be tolerant and accepting.

46

Protecting your kids-- dealing with abuse.

Your primary job as a parent is to protect your children. If you suspect abuse, you must act. This can be physical, emotional, or even sexual abuse. Seek the help of a counselor. Do not let your children ride in a car with an intoxicated person. You may have to seek court intervention in such cases. Your children depend on you to act.

47

What about the rights of grandparents?

The United States Supreme Court has ruled that grandparents have no rights if there is a living, fit parent. Parenting plans sometimes have provisions for grand-parent visits but it is up to the parents to include this. If neither parent is fit, grandparents may seek third party custody or temporary guardianship.

48

You can accommodate different parenting styles.

Often parents have different parenting styles. Some are more hands-on and strict and others more easygoing. One may have strict dietary rules and the other is a fast-food parent. Unless there is a genuine safety or health concern, each parent must respect the rules of the other household.

49

Parenting evaluator: why you need one.

If there are genuine health and safety concerns with the other parent, a parenting evaluator may be necessary. This can be court-appointed or agreed upon. The evaluator may request psychological evaluations of both parents. This can become expensive and intrusive. The evaluator may recommend phased-in parenting plans after a parent has completed certain programs.

50

Weddings, graduations. Who gets to go?

The goal of a grownup divorce is that everyone can attend future life events. There should be no concern about who goes to the graduations, weddings, and births of the grandchildren. Even as new partners appear, they should all be part of the family. Grandchildren can't have too many loving grandparents.

Money, Money. The Root of Problems

51

Gathering the assets, do your homework.

Now that you have filed, it is time to gather assets. Try to find bank and credit card statements, tax returns and any other financial statements. Ask your pension plan or retirement account administrator to provide statements. Don't worry if you can't find everything. Your spouse will be required to provide documents as well. Get a copy of your credit report. There can be valuable information there.

52

Determining separate property, what is it?

Anything acquired during the marriage is community property. Separate property is anything you had before marriage or got as a gift or inheritance. Personal injury awards that relate to pain and suffering are also separate. You will need to provide tracing. If you comingled, you may not be able to claim separate property.

53

Stock awards, bonuses, options, oh my!

These can be complicated and you may want to use a specialist to determine values. Stock awards may not be vested but may have a community component. Bonuses are determined to be community by when they were earned, not awarded. A bonus may be for a period from July to June but not paid until September. Date of separation is important in this case.

54

Informal discovery and when you escalate.

Most divorces are completed with "informal discovery" and the parties voluntarily provide needed information. In many marriages, both parties are fully aware of the extent of their assets and can easily fill out a spread sheet. If you are concerned your spouse is not forthcoming then you may need to go to "formal discovery."

55

Subpoena, deposition, interrogatories. What are they?

There are many tools your lawyer uses for formal discovery. Bank accounts and employment records can be obtained by subpoena. Interrogatories are questions that must be answered under oath and a party can be found in contempt of court for not answering completely. A party can also be examined under oath at deposition in front of a court reporter.

56

Community property; who is on title?

Community property is any property acquired during the marriage, regardless of who is on title. This is true of real estate, vehicles, bank accounts and retirement accounts. Credit cards are also community debt, no matter whose name is on the card. Gifts and inheritance are separate and should be kept in separate accounts, not comingled.

57

Self-employed or family business challenges

Self-employed or sole proprietorships face special challenges as it can be difficult to determine the actual income, or the value of the business. A business valuation is often necessary to determine the value of the business. The taxable income may be very different from the actual income as many small businesses pay for personal expenses out of the business.

58

Certified Divorce Financial Analyst-- forensic accountant

A Certified Divorce Financial Analyst (CDFA) can be very useful in helping you determine an equitable financial settlement. They can do projections as to where each party will be years in the future. They can help set budgets for support and evaluate tax consequences. A forensic accountant is useful in determining if money had been misappropriated.

59

Can we just do this informally?

Of course you can. Most couples are both informed as to the extent of their assets and can cooperate on an equitable division of property. There are not formal requirements if both parties agree that all property and assets have been disclosed. In these cases, if either side's attorney is insisting on formal discovery, one might question the attorney's motivation.

60

Is my spouse hiding any money?

If your spouse is a W-2 employee it is very hard to hide money. There is usually a tracing of money withdrawn from a bank account. Tax returns have 1099s from financial accounts. Self-employed, small businesses may have more opportunity to hide money but a good forensic accountant can help. Cayman Island accounts are rare and not that easy to obtain.

Child Support is
for the Kids

No support if parenting time equal?

There is a popular myth that if parenting time is equal there is no child support. This is not true. Child support is based on the relative income of the parties. There may be an adjustment for significant time with the other parent but it depends on whether there is sufficient income in the other home to provide for the children.

62

How do we calculate child support?

Washington State has a child support calculator which provides guideline support. It is based upon each parent's income. Spousal maintenance is counted as income in the calculation. The amount can vary depending on tax exemptions. Also, extraordinary needs can be considered. Adjustment can also be made if children are with the other parent for a significant amount of time.

63

If parent chooses to quit work.

If a parent quits work and chooses not to work, the court will consider this voluntary unemployment and will "impute" income, generally at the level parent was earning historically. Adjustments can be made if a parent loses a job for no fault. A court can require a spouse to provide monthly reports of effort to obtain employment.

64

Imputed income for under-employed spouse.

Sometimes if a spouse is not working full-time, a court may "impute" income to full-time. Some professions, however, consider a 32-hour work week full-time. Someone with a history of high earnings choosing a low wage job may be imputed at a higher amount. There is a federal income table for earnings based on age and gender, which are quite low.

65

Who pays for the extracurricular activities?

Agreed-upon extracurricular activities and private schools are above child support and are allocated proportionally by each party's earnings. Even if not agreed upon, if the child has habitually been engaging in those activities, a court might order to continue them. Some parents choose to simply raise the child support amount so they don't have to do accounting.

66

What if parent does not pay?

There are severe sanctions for not paying child support. Professional licenses, driver's licenses and government employment can be withheld if a parent is behind on child support. In some cases a parent can be jailed. These arrears cannot be discharged in bankruptcy and go well beyond the child's age of majority. A grown child can sue for back child support.

67

Adjusting for extraordinarily high-income parents.

The support schedules top out at a certain point for household income. Provisions can be made for higher income but it is not automatic and the court requires "findings" showing that the children are used to a higher cost lifestyle. Most higher income parents agree on an amount considered "above guideline."

68

How long does child support last?

Child support covers food, shelter, and clothing but not extracurricular activities or out-of-pocket medical costs. It lasts until the child turns eighteen or completes high school, whichever is later. A child over eighteen must be enrolled in school full-time and making satisfactory progress. Some parents agree to extend child support until the start of college.

69

Does child support include college costs?

Child support does not include college costs but often the court will expect parents to make provision for college if the parents have college degrees. The child is expected to provide a portion and the parents share proportionally by their income. The parents are only expected to provide at the state university standard. The exact provisions may be deferred for later.

Spousal Maintenance-- Alimony by Another Name

70

Alimony, how much for how long?

Spousal support is based upon "need and ability to pay." There is no exact calculator and it is based upon many factors such as the length of the marriage, the earning history and capability of each spouse. There is no formula for length of time. The parties' ages, career history, and future earning ability are all factors. Gender is not a factor.

71

What about marital standard of living?

While marital standard of living may be a factor, it is well established that most divorcing couples cannot maintain this standard. Both parties are expected to become self-supporting. In the case of an older retired couple, it is expected that both parties should be equally situated. Length of the marriage is also a factor.

72

Should I go back to school?

If you can show that additional education can improve your earning capacity, that is an excellent idea. If you show how long the program is, what the income and job opportunities are, you might be able to get support for a longer period and not be expected to be employed.

73

Can I be charged imputed income?

If you are not working, working only part-time, or working at less than you have made historically, the court might impute income to a certain amount. This can be alleviated by showing employment is no longer available in your field, that the hours you are working are standard in the industry, or that you have health issues preventing you from work.

74

What are tax consequences of alimony?

Alimony is taxable income to the person receiving it and deductible to the person paying it. This can be a strategy for reducing the tax obligations of the couple by shifting incomes from the high earner to the lower earner in a lower bracket. You should consider how much you must pay in taxes when considering your living expenses.

75

What if my spouse is unemployed?

This can be challenging. Why is your spouse unemployed? Health reasons? A stay-at-home parent who has never worked? It is possible that your spouse may be expected to seek employment eventually or income may be imputed. There might be spousal support for a while that has a step down (or up) later.

76

Why not consider undifferentiated family support?

Undifferentiated family support combines child support and spousal maintenance. For IRS purposes, it is treated as income to the recipient and can be deducted by the payor. This can be an excellent tax strategy, but must be properly written to comply with tax law. This is an especially useful tool if one of the parties has substantially higher income.

Are men and women treated equally?

Theoretically the courts are gender blind. In reality, this isn't always so. For example, a man seems to have a higher burden in seeking spousal maintenance. A way to judge bias is to present the same facts only reverse gender. Under this standard, high earning women would pay spousal support as often as high earning men.

78

What are consequences of inherited wealth?

Inherited wealth is separate property but can be a factor in determining spousal maintenance. A spouse with inherited wealth will have a lesser need. Similarly, a spouse who has significant assets may have more ability to pay. In Washington State, all property is before the court and the court is required to make an "equitable" finding.

79

Can spousal maintenance be changed later?

If a court orders spousal maintenance, it is modifiable with a showing of "substantial change of circumstances." Most couples, in negotiating their settlement agreement, make tradeoffs in property division and spousal maintenance and therefore want the spousal maintenance to be non-modifiable. This must be spelled out in the settlement agreement.

Community Property: What Does that Mean?

80

Who's on title is not determinative.

Washington is a community property state. Community property is any property, real or personal, acquired during the marriage. This includes real estate and bank and retirement accounts, no matter whose name is on the title. The exception is anything acquired by gift, inheritance or sometimes proceeds from a personal injury lawsuit, provided proof is available.

81

Determining premarital assets and comingled assets.

Assets owned prior to marriage are considered separate property. Retirement accounts can generally be easy to trace. Financial accounts can become so comingled they are no longer recognizable as separate property and may be considered gift to community. Real estate transactions likewise can become convoluted. The better the paper trail, the easier it is to identify separate property.

82

Inheritance, gifts, and loans from family.

Often a couple has received gifts or loans from family. The question becomes whether the gift was made to the individual or to the couple. Sometimes the intent can be determined by documents such as gift cards or letters. Inheritance is easily identified by the decedent's will. In both cases, comingling can become problematic. Were the funds kept in separate accounts?

83

How to divide pensions, retirement accounts

Pensions are rare these days. They are a guarantee of future income at a certain age. Retirement accounts include IRAs and 401Ks and have account statements showing value. Retirement accounts can be rolled over into the nonparticipant's account. Pensions and 401Ks require a Qualified Domestic Relations Order (QDRO). IRAs can be divided by the administrator based on a Decree of Settlement agreement.

Stock awards, bonuses, and employment perks.

Bonuses can have a community property component based upon the employment period they were awarded, not when actually received. Stock awards may have "vesting schedules," and a forensic accountant can help determine value, or at least next vesting period after separation. One should also look at other employment perks. Some might be property or might be considered income.

85

When an unequal division is equitable.

Even though Washington is a community property state, community property is divided on "equitable" principles. This can result in one spouse receiving greater than fifty percent if it is deemed that the other spouse will continue to build wealth but the other will not. Sometimes a spouse will get a greater share of the property instead of spousal maintenance.

86

How a spreadsheet is your friend

A spreadsheet can help you determine a reasonable property settlement. You don't necessarily divide everything down the middle. Put assets and debts in different columns and move them around to receive the desirable outcome. You might put the house in one column and move other assets around. You should include all types of assets, including vehicles, and even a value for household goods.

87

How to value a family business

It is important to get a value on a family business or professional services firm. While the business may go entirely to the person running it, the property division should include a value for the business. A professional business evaluator is necessary for this. Sometimes a bank will require a business valuation for lending purposes. This could be a starting point.

88

Household items, furniture and other "stuff"

Find a way to divide household items, tools, and furniture yourself. One way is to use colored dots. Each person can put a dot on each item they want. Then see if there are things you both want. Find a way to resolve that. In extreme cases, folks bring in professional arbitrator which is expensive. These items are valued at garage sale prices.

89

Family pets are the other children.

While technically family pets are considered personal property, they often are more than that and have great emotional value. Folks have gone to court over their pets. There are no easy answers, but you may consider a version of a parenting plan for pets. Some people even provide "pet support" provisions.

You Did It! Getting Final Decree

90

Ways to get to amicable agreement

Ninety-nine percent of cases settle out of court, so why not try an amicable approach? Find attorney websites that support non-adversarial resolution. Washington State Bar Association rules prohibit "dual" representation. Some attorneys offer a "one attorney" model. If you choose a mediator it should be an attorney, or consider collaborative law, which has specific protocols.

91

Mediation, settlement conference, arbitration, or trial

There are two types of mediation. *Interest-based* is effective early on in negotiations. In *Evaluative,* the mediator gives an opinion on your case and what a judge might do. These are generally used for settlement conferences which are often required before cases can go to trial. Trials are very formal and most cases settle well before trial.

92

Maybe you do need a judge.

While almost all cases settle without trial, sometimes it is necessary to let a judge decide. If your spouse will not agree with anything, even though attorneys have explained the law, you may need a judge to finally give a ruling. Remember, judges must abide by existing case law and cannot be persuaded by your compelling story.

93

Your spouse has disappeared, now what?

There are several ways to achieve proper "service" if your spouse has disappeared. These include service by mail or publication, which requires a court order and the careful following of proper procedure. If your spouse does not respond, you may get your decree by "default." You cannot get anything by default that you did not ask for in the petition, so plan ahead.

94

Preserve privacy with marital settlement agreement.

Everything you put in court documents is public record. You can put your financial settlement in a Marital Settlement Agreement (MSA) which is a contract not filed with the court. Your final decree will reference the agreement including language that "all property and debt has been divided in accordance with a marital settlement agreement." It is a fully enforceable court order.

95

Change your name, it's your decision.

You get a free name change with your divorce decree. Yes, men can also request one. It is your decision and your spouse has no say about whether you keep your name. The name you choose does not have to be a name you've used before. You can choose any name you want, perhaps choosing to reinvent yourself with a different name.

96

Making sure your agreement is enforceable.

Review your agreement to make sure there are no loose ends. Be specific about time frames. (Not "when he can afford it.") Real property should be properly described. It is a good idea to include provisions in case your spouse files for bankruptcy. Remember that even though debts are assigned to your spouse, the creditor is not bound by your agreement.

97

Qualified Domestic Relations Order, it's important.

Pensions and 401K retirement accounts are divided by Qualified Domestic Relations Orders (QDRO) (pronounced "quadro"). The plan administrator can provide a template. The order must be signed by a judge and then presented to the plan. This is a step people forget until retirement or the death of a spouse, when it is too late to fix.

98

The last step: your divorce decree

Your divorce is final when a judge signs it. In many cases you do not need to go to court, but this varies by county in Washington. Your decree is public record so it should not list your financial accounts which should be divided in a marital settlement agreement. If you are changing names be sure to get a "certified" decree.

99

How to enforce the settlement agreement

Even though your marital settlement agreement has not been entered with the court, it is as enforceable as a court order. If the agreement was carefully crafted there should be no ambiguities. When there is disagreement as to terms, or one party does not cooperate, you can get court assistance and your spouse can even be held in contempt of court!

100

You did it!
Start your future.

Some people like to have their friends help them in a divorce party or ritual for closure. You will also want to make sure to complete title transfers, change account names and change your name on documents such as your Social Security card, passport and others. You will probably receive electronic copies of your documents to keep when needed. Make it a good new life.

About the Six-Word Lessons Series

Legend has it that Ernest Hemingway was challenged to write a story using only six words. He responded with the story, "For sale: baby shoes, never worn." The story tickles the imagination. Why were the shoes never worn? The answers are left up to the reader's imagination.

This style of writing has a number of aliases: postcard fiction, flash fiction, and micro fiction. Lonnie Pacelli was introduced to this concept in 2009 by a friend, and started thinking about how this extreme brevity could apply to today's communication culture of text messages, tweets and Facebook posts. He wrote the first book, *Six-Word Lessons for Project Managers*, then started helping other authors write and publish their own books in the series.

The books all have six-word chapters with six-word lesson titles, each followed by a one-page description. They can be written by entrepreneurs who want to promote their businesses, or anyone with a message to share.

See the entire *Six-Word Lessons Series* at
6wordlessons.com